VOICE: POEMS

VOICE: POEMS
BY ALLISON JOSEPH

MAYAPPLE PRESS 2009

Published by   MAYAPPLE PRESS
              408 N. Lincoln St.
              Bay City, MI 48708
              www.mayapplepress.com

ISBN 978-0932412-75-1

ACKNOWLEDGMENTS

Emergency Librarian: *DorothyPrizes.org* (Dorothy Sargent Rosenberg Prizes website); Pedestrian's Blues: *Free Lunch*; Elegy for My Father's Anger: *Peninsula Poets*, Poetry Society of Michigan; Tourist Attraction: *Hotmetalpress.com*; Melancholia: *Alalitcom*; Prompt, To the DJ Who Played the Isley Brothers' "Between the Sheets" on a Monday Morning, My Husband Plays Me Marley, Eating Out: *Tamaqua*; Professor Apathy: *The Ledge*; Whiner's Lounge: *Atlanta Review*; Extraction: *The Litchfield Review*

Cover art courtesy www.cepolina.com. Cover designed by Judith Kerman. Book designed and typset by Amee Schmidt with titles in Lithos Pro and text in Candara.

CONTENTS

Fear of a Performance Poet

You sit in trepidation, fearing
what she might do, how she
might touch you, turn you inside

out, upside down, leave you gasping
for breath and struggling for foothold.
She might just undress you, upbraid

you, scold you with bitterness
and scald you in beauty. Ice
under your fingertips, rage under

your eyelids, she drizzles salt in the cuts
she has scored in the flesh of each
and every one of your backs.

She is a bruise you cannot resist—
you lean forward for her blows and like
it, want it, her tongue the lash,

her mouth the origin, first orifice.
Her words are worry beads, prayer beads,
beats of sorrow and beats that sweat.

Not berry-sweet or candy-colored,
not cinnamon and honey, she's copper—
hard but able to bend, to shine,

to wrap like wire around your wrists,
your throat, glinting with a keener luster
than anything you've ever owned.

VOICE

Nothing as naked as the human voice—
its cries of pain or pleasure, the whisper
meant for you alone, the scream

as flesh is slapped and startled
into submission, the agony of the moment
you hear your beloved is gone, crushed,

unable to reside in your arms again,
and you wail, pound fists on the walls,
no coming up and out of you before

you can stop it. Consider its registers,
its hues, its tonal acrobatics,
love of syncopation and lullabies.

Scratchy, throaty, husky, meek,
nasal, high-pitched, low-pitched,
full of gravity or gravel, smoke

or grease. When you hear my voice,
you don't have to know anything
about me to know I love

the motion of words through air,
sound waves punctuated by breath, a music
each one of us is capable of making.

KNITTING

Stitch by stitch, I am knitting
back into my life, needles clicking
point by point, skein after skein
unraveling at my feet, unspooling
like days, like the rhythms
I had lost before my hands
took up this art again,
art of my mother—whose
homemade sweater still
warms me now, long after
her fingers have gone to bone,
art of generations of women
who knitted us into afghans
and scarves, hats and socks.
Yes, it is both craft and
art, skill and legacy—
twisting, unwinding,
casting on, binding off.
Relearning this, I'm
learning to knit two
together, to pull rows
apart, ripping fabric
back to my error then
knitting it all back up again.
Maybe this time, I'll knit
you into warmth, into dream,
pillow I've made beneath
your head, a shawl warming
your shoulders, each stitch
a lucky enduring kiss.

SOMETHING ABOUT HOTEL ROOMS

makes me write poetry, makes me long
for syllables under my breath or counted

on my fingers, anything to stop the deadening
of the blank bed with its funeral corners,

of the mass-produced pictures of flowers
smug in pastel frames. Something about

a room for rent and me alone makes words
elusive at other times, other hours, come

tumbling forth, inky on scraps of hotel
stationary, backs of take-out menus.

Something about a strange city and a
hotel full of conventioneers hawking

beauty products and swapping business cares
makes me retreat to utterance, malice of

a literary kind, contempt I never have
to share. Something about rescuing myself

with my own hands and these plastic hotel
pens, something about holding onto what

brought me this far—that's what makes me
write poetry—not the dim disdainful smile

of the concierge, not the pity of the front
desk clerk when she inquires how many

room keys I'll need and I say one,
my solitary bags asleep at my feet.

EMERGENCY LIBRARIAN

Does she speed up in an ambulance
or a bookmobile? Or does she dash
into neglected neighborhood classrooms,
clad in white coat, sensible shoes, yelling

get that boy a paperback stat!, snatching
video games out of sweaty clutches
with a single grab? Teachers call her
when no ordinary bookwrangler will do,

confident she'll make readers of the most
illiterate, the most belligerent, the bored
and sullen. With her, story hour never
ends, and her stories send a child around

the world and back, a fluid fluency
of dialect and custom, alphabets
and hieroglyphs. Instead of a stethoscope,
she wields a cart laden with books,

literary miracle worker, woman who gets
the most hostile child to love reading,
eager to teach what he's learned to another
new reader, the shyest girl reaching

for the brightest picture book, moving
from easy readers to eighth-grade level
in a single afternoon. She can never
feed them enough language, enough

characters, for they are always
wanting more from this sorceress,
this priestess, a conjure woman of words
in bifocals and turtleneck sweater.

NAÏVE QUESTIONS

Why call it ethnic cleansing when nothing
ever gets clean, landscapes replete
with slaughtered bodies? Why talk
of domestic violence, as if violence
deserves a home, can be tamed like weeds,
like a snarling animal? Why call people
who make up most of the world
minorities? Why speak of the electoral
college when no one can pass an entrance
exam, pay tuition, and then attend?
Will an electoral university replace
this vexed college? And who will lead
this university in this era of double-digit
budget cuts? Why capital punishment
and corporal punishment, but not corporate
punishment? Why do those put on paid
leave never actually leave, hold news
conferences instead, declaring innocence
to the press, who can't press anyone
to answer anything? Why call people
who damage children pedophile, when phile
means lover—bibliophile, audiophile, Anglophile?
Why do menopause and menstruation contain
men—isn't meningitis enough? Can people be
biracial when there's one human race?
And if we're only human, all created equal,
how can there be a Supreme Court?

EXTRACTION

If there's a poem in you, get it out
by any means necessary—use pliers
if you must, or grab it with your bare
hands and pull, dislodging stony roots,
thorny bushes. Don't let that poem
hunker beneath your skin, unsaid,
unshed, stuck between bones or
swallowed. If it's too weak to come
out, too fluttery and unstable, feed
yourself lines from other, stronger
poems until your poem grows thick-
thighed, sable-tongued, ready to strut,
sultry, agile. If your poem is minnow-
slippery, just as quick, you must move
quickly too, casting your net wide
but not letting your poem tangle
in its nylon. No excuses when a poem
burgeons, nascent, budding on the cusp
of your lips, terrace of your tongue.
Don't let that poem sail from you,
send you a postcard later. Go get it
now, before it scurries away,
scattering words in its wake.

PEDESTRIAN'S BLUES

Please don't run me over with your big red car;
slow down and give a woman walking room.
My feet may be tired, but I've traveled this far.

Put down that phone, that blunt hand-rolled cigar.
Slow down and don't send me to certain doom.
Please don't run me over with your big blue car—

stay home to drink, no skidding from a bar
into a vehicle, in nightdark gloom.
My feet may be tired, but I've traveled this far,

with so much more work to do—learn my guitar,
write poetry that no one else will groom.
Please don't run me over with your big green car:

remember how sedate some of us are;
we don't move quickly, slower now to bloom.
My feet may be tired, but I've traveled this far,

pebbles in my shoes, soles dark with asphalt, tar.
Don't make this narrow street my end, my tomb.
My feet may be tired, but I've traveled this far.
Please don't run me down with your big new car.

TOURIST ATTRACTION

Come play in my graceland;
take a long, slow dip in my
reflecting pool, patriotic and

aroused all at once. Come climb
my monuments, all the way
up my arch and back down again,

for truly, I am the gateway
to the west. Take a trip to my
empire state building, where

the observation deck is always
packed, teeming with warmth
and a certain giddy dizziness

that comes with profound heights.
Tour my zoos, urban menageries full
of fins and feathers, downy nests

and botanical wonders—flora, fauna,
footprints. For you, I'm the painted
desert, the fruited plain, the streetcar,

subway, the El and tube, the English
channel and the Ivory Coast. Universal,
I'm the great adventure, rollercoaster

with so many happy loops
you scream when you finally
plunge down, get off. For you,

I'm waiting, open, no
lines at my ticket booths,
no charge at my welcome gates.

FULL MEAL DEAL

after "Milkshake," as recorded by Kelis

If your milkshake brings all the boys
to the yard, what about the rest

of the meal: leafy greens or savory bites
of meat, fish—braised or baked or boiled?

What about bread that rises only
to be consumed with butter or jam,

what about fluffy lemon cake with cream
icing, smooth going, rapture-sweet?

What about your sides—rice with gravy,
mac and cheese, potatoes any way you like?

That shake you sell may be tasty,
but if it's the only meal you offer,

we'll all surely starve, lack of nourishment
making us all less than we can be, a poor

collective. So let me show you some more
recipes, a panoply of courses from a

five star chef, anything anyone
would want to taste on my menu.

WHINER'S LOUNGE

Everyone is welcome at the Whiner's Lounge—
no complaint too large or too small, no pet peeve
or lawsuit ignored, open 24 hours, seven days,

and staffed by waitresses with plump arms,
abundant smiles, elderly grandpas as bus boys,
smelling of tobacco and wisdom. Everyone here

cares about what burden makes your shoulders
sag, and if you want to whine, cry, moan, scream,
stare into space or doodle your name on multiple

placemats, no one will stop or chide you.
No one says *suck it up or you don't have it
so bad or don't be a wuss.* Go ahead,

the waitresses and grandpas say, be a wuss,
keen and wail all night if you have to.
When you're done crying, we'll bring you

a giant sundae, mountains of ice cream
with hot fudge, as many cherries on top
as you want. So you sit at the counter,

sink your head onto folded arms,
and let loose tears that you don't have
to justify, hot regret gilding your face.

REALLY MEAN GIRLS

They leave you bleeding in a heap,
crushed at the bottom of a stairwell,
gold chain ripped off your neck,

brand new leather coat snatched
off your back. They puncture
new whitewalls, scratch keys

through the sheen of a fresh
paint job, BITCH carved so deep
no touch-up can repair the impact.

Why they despise you
is up for debate: your eyes,
hair, skin, face, curves, charms,

breasts, hips, thighs. They don't
want to get to know you better;
they'd prefer you wiped from the earth,

extinct as an Edsel, just as popular.
High heels and fake nails
are their weapons, and while

their words, spat at you in
the cafeteria or locker room,
hurt, what hurts most are the scars

they leave, black and blue
bruises on virgin skin,
pummelings from six fists

at once, broken sutures
that never heal right until
you leave school for good.

MELANCHOLIA

Much better than ordinary misery
or clinical depression, melancholy
comes robed in rose silk,
glissando piano fingerings

accompanying her arrival,
her visit the one you wait for
long after bliss and bitterness
have left, before resignation,

withdrawal. She shimmers,
talks of cocktails and torch songs,
hovers above you like a shroud,
a cloak she shares with you only—

her now passenger, her equal.
She's blues before the real blues come,
erudite and sophisticated, queen
of the soft focus lens, paper lantern.

She's a chameleon, a chanteuse,
and you can't stop looking at wells
of sorrow she calls eyes, blue shadows
beneath. With her here, your songs

are that much deeper, arias too beautiful
to be listless, sadness colored indigo
and chartreuse, vermilion and verdigris.
When she leaves, you loathe the flavorless

drone who replaces her, a temp worker
on 9 to 5 payroll, no more shimmerings
in indigo night, no more hazy visage
staring back at you, mouthing your name.

PROFESSOR INSCRUTABLE

Writes poetry that no one comprehends.
Drops theory down your throat until you drown.
Makes you watch films in foreign languages
without subtitles or a study guide.

Drops theory down your throat until you drown;
wears black to every dour somber class.
Without subtitles or a study guide,
she thinks you'll learn a lifetime's worth of text.

Wears black to every dour somber class.
Insults you to your face when you speak out.
He thinks you'll learn a lifetime's worth of text
in seminars that meet just once a week.

Insults you to your face when you speak out,
but mocks you if you're quiet, thoughtful, tense.
In seminars that meet just once a week,
she talks about herself incessantly.

He mocks you if you're quiet, thoughtful, tense,
each paper that you write worse than the last.
He talks about himself incessantly,
digressing though nobody asked him to.

Each paper that you write worse than the last,
you've given up on her, on him, this school.
Digressing though nobody asked her to,
her cryptic speeches mystify us all.

You've given up on her, on him, this school,
on films you watched in foreign languages.
His cryptic speeches mystifying all, he
writes poetry that no one comprehends.

SHOPPING LIST

Buy me some bass lines,
funky and thick, sweaty
as the small of your back
on a summer afternoon.

Buy me some drums—
not the drums themselves
but their sounds: conga
thump, snare drum snap.

Don't forget guitar; I need
a lot of that: acoustic,
electric, Delta swamp song
and Chicago boogie, I need

both and more, like barrelhouse
piano, hot licks played
quick but raunchy, foot-
stomping bass that wiggles

hips before they know it,
taking up permanent residence
in the pelvis, solar plexus,
the nexus of where we stir,

and live, restless, tempted.
Deliver me tight beats—
ripe and ready to rip,
sonic boom inside each one.

Slip me some back-up too—
vocal yeahs, all rights,
and amens, adlibbing,
freestyling, stone cold vamping.

Total that up and send
me the bill—I'll gladly
pay for music I can't
make any other way.

To the DJ Who Played the Isley Brothers' "Between the Sheets" on a Monday Morning

How am I supposed to drag myself from bed
when this song is cooing me back in?
Bleary-eyed before showering, eating,
I still stop, sway to this slow, sinuous groove,
a song that makes a body wish for satin,
full champagne flutes, incense, body oils—
baby-making music. This is not
what I need at 6:23 a.m. if I'm
to get out the door to make any money;
like another Isley song says, I've got work
to do, I've got a job, baby. I can't
be standing here, caught up in Ronnie's
close-the-bedroom door voice,
a voice like a plea and a prayer all at once.
At least play "Fight the Power,"
get me psyched up to confront the world.
What will you play next? "Sexual Healing?"
"Pillow Talk?" Are you trying to make
the whole city swoon back into bed
until you go off the air, and we've
blown the entire day on pleasures
the best of us will have to sing about?

EATING OUT

Don't you love that moment
when they place the menu before you,
all your choices spelled out

in details of tarragon
or fennel, star anise or
roasted chile? I love

that moment too when the waiter
goes through his litany of specials:
the curried, poached, glazed,

drizzled, blackened, sauced,
blanched, broasted, one-day-only,
sorry-we've-run-out-of-that-dish

dishes, the candied, sinful
chocolate-rich, crème-de-menthe,
devil's food, strawberry-sauced

and raspberry-tarted desserts.
It's like the orgasm before
the orgasm, the minor ripple

that precedes the blast
your body knows as full pleasure.
So go ahead, order the soup,

let its creamy warmth slide
over your tongue in pursuit
of the apt taste buds,

have the appetizer: white
cheese and olive oil softening
the crusty coat of bread wedges.

Taste something you've never had,
can't pronounce: enoki mushrooms,
arugula, crème fraiche, herb velouté.

Eat slowly, for you did not
cook this yourself, nor
did someone hand it to you

in a paper bag with plastic forks.
Don't just chew, but lick, savor,
your tongue caressing the roof

of your mouth, flavors you've hoped
for all week finally here, flooding
your mouth. When you're sated, sigh.

MY HUSBAND PLAYS ME MARLEY

more than any white man born and bred in Arkansas
should, so much that I think any day now
he will wake with a head full of dreads,
big spliff between his lips like Marley's
on the album covers. In this age of mp3s,
he actually owns the albums, even the one
when the cover tells you how to clean herb.
Though I'm the one with the mother from Jamaica,
he's the one leading me through "Get Up, Stand Up,"
and "Rastaman Vibration." I guess that makes me
Rita to his Bob, and I'm so glad to sing with him,
to give thanks and praises to a god I wouldn't
refer to otherwise. He makes me name each Wailer,
fills me with stories of Bunny and Peter Tosh
(Bunny could sing while Peter talked his way
through a song), marvels with me at how much
Ziggy looks like his dad, even if the younger Marley
isn't nearly as astonishing musically.
I think Bob would smile if he knew us,
laughing at my husband even though he's
a "crazy baldhead," a white man like the white captain
who married Marley's eighteen-year-old mother,
only sent money after their son was born.
When my husband croons, "No Woman, No Cry,"
he changes the words, sings the name of our town
instead of Trench Town, and I begin to think I could live
anywhere with him, any place we can open windows,
drapes, let in a pale imitation of the sun Marley knew.
Nowhere we can go where Marley can't follow,
singing sweet songs, melodies clear and true.
This is Marley's message to us, and we
are grateful this messenger once walked this earth,
telling us every little thing is gonna be alright.
And we listen, dance to his voice in the light of our lives.

PROFESSOR APATHY

No office hours ever. If you don't understand
what we talked about in class, too bad. I'm
not here to make sure you get it. I'm not here
to care about whether you are enlightened,

educated, or entertained. I'm here for my research,
and teaching is the lowest possible priority for me,
cast down there with clipping my toenails or
taking my car to Jiffy Lube, which is where

you'll be working because I don't care if you
pass this class, if you've read the chapters prior
to the mid-term, the final, the quiz, surprise quiz
that I've given for ten years running because I

don't care to make any new ones. I don't care
if there aren't enough handouts to go around,
if the Xeroxes are too blurry to read, if my
writing on the blackboard looks like chicken

scratch, if you can't hear me because I don't
speak loudly enough, won't project, won't wear
a mic even though the department owns one
I could borrow because that would mean I'd

have to go find it, and I don't go find anything
that will make school easier for you. Because
I don't care now that I've got tenure. Not
that I did before, but I don't need to pretend

anymore. I don't have to do
anything except stay bored and die,
your hands shivering in air as you try
to ask questions I will never answer.

DON'T

Don't be fingering my sugar
unless you want to taste my salt,
teasing my honey then ignoring
my bitter, satisfied with a simple

taste of sweetness uncomplicated
by tang, by sour, by vinegar
that clarifies as it cleans.
Don't grab my bottle, drink

my liqueur, then replace it
when you feel like it, slipping me
peach brandy when I sip
crème de menthe. Don't page

my book with slippery hands,
splatter grease on sheets
I haven't read or slept on,
leaving stains I can't get out.

Don't undo my hooks and eyes
until you set your own zipper
straight, your buttons
lined up with the right holes,

snaps set into their grooves
until I decide otherwise.
Come correct, then maybe
I'll let you graze my grain,

sweep my floor, brush
of fingertip pleasure
soft enough to stir my dead,
firm enough to make them sleep again.

WHAT THE ELDERS TELL YOU

When your parents have died
and their friends are still living,
they sit you down and tell you
everything you didn't know
and everything you half-suspected

about them, all the affirmations
and confirmations you'd been
waiting for for so many years.
They are your elders still,
but now you are an adult,

maybe with children of your own,
certainly with bills and mortgages,
debts collapsing your expectations, hopes.
Because you are old now too,
these elders tell you of all

your parents' transgressions:
the adultery, the drinking,
the fractured friendships they never
mended, redeemed only with
their dying. The elders lean forward

as they tell you these things,
laughing with unfamiliar relish
as they recollect their friends,
shaking heads in disapproval
at the misdeeds of the dead.

But did you want to know
your parents were human?
Weren't you planning
on mourning them forever,
stuck at the age you were

when they died, never reconciling
their adult lives with yours?
Questions tumble from you faster
than you can open your mouth,
and the elders, with their

shaky hands and graying temples,
answer each one—not the veiled
dismissals of your youth,
not with the sly winks
and nudges that did not

include you then,
but with the truth,
salacious and bitter and
humorous, broken
in ways you never expected.

Do Me the Favor of

not asking me for a reference, a recommendation,
an assessment of your remarkable worth to all
future employers. I don't have the words

to make you better than you are, the phrases
to get you chosen from the pile, anointed
above all others, touched by whatever greatness

you want or think you deserve. Do me the favor
of not turning me into a liar, a re-seller
of shopworn superlatives, an administrator

of wishes that cannot be granted by a missive
on official stationary. No matter the typeface
on your expensive resume paper, no matter

how obsequious the prose of your letter
to the head of human resources, I will not
make a way out of no way for you,

will not ease your entry into a world
you haven't proved you're ready for.
Do me the favor of leaving,

and don't come back until
you've earned the right to have
my praise light you up from the inside out,

a glow I can write about without
lining my mouth with falsehoods, without
swallowing the hard lump of my own disgust.

PROMPT

Write me a poem about
the last good barroom brawl
you witnessed, how the patrons
spilled out of their seats
at the smack of fists on flesh.
Write me a poem about
the last peacock you saw—
how the sly unfolding of feathers
could still stop you as you pivoted
through the zoo, balloon
in one hand, three-year-old
in the other. Write me a poem
as loud and dissonant
as the county orchestra tuning up,
lazy as the lisp your cousin
didn't relinquish until eighth grade.
Write something to keep me awake
long after nightfall, with lines
that will lodge in my head so fiercely
a month will have to pass
before I can breathe again.
Write me a poem that smokes,
that leaves ashes in my bed,
thumbprints on my skin.
Write a poem for me
with your shoulders, backbone,
a poem that can hold the brusque
angles of elbows, sleepy cast
of eyelids. Write me a poem
and make it so fine
that I'll want it more
than my own poems,
my own breath and blood.

ELEGY FOR MY FATHER'S ANGER

Goodbye to the crazed roar that came
from him, the hazy heat that did not cool
with age, rank speech from his lips that cut me
harder than his belt or his hand. How anger

ate at him, taut as an itch, a peril I invoked
with airy sass and backtalk, failures in class,
with notions I voiced in luxury of ignorance,
unaware I'd tempted his ancient ire, a black

man's bitterness unslaked, despite my mother's
prayers, her whispered comfort. No cup or light
could soothe the punch of his raised voice, the reek
and slap of his every accusation, his hunches that

we'd done him wrong, made him poor.
He'd roam the rooms of our house, slamming
doors off their latches, out of reach until he turned
on us, easy targets. Though you are long dead,

Father, your madness lingers, attends me in
dreams, faithful as assets accruing interest.
I hear you hit bottom each time I catch a vision
of myself at nine, notches of your belt hitting

the arch of my backside, its elegant curve
wrecked as an alley. And should I speak of this again,
your passion spent for naught except my nighmares?
I try to kick myself free of this: my inheritance, your gift.

THE COST

after Dorothy Parker's "Ballade at Thirty-Five"

This, no song of a cranky witch,
this, no saga sweetly sung.
This, no played-out movie pitch,
no demo for the hip and young.
I've come unwrapped, been tightly strung.
I've railed at inequality,
climbed ladders with unsteady rungs.
No woman gets through life for free.

This, no chant of an angry bitch,
This, no treatise newly sprung.
I've had due time to soothe each itch;
I've swung some bells, and had mine swung,
worn out my hands, my eyes, my tongue,
been addled by my history,
cracked pieces I have dwelled among.
No woman gets through life for free.

I've had my years to writhe and twitch,
those days when air seeped from my lungs,
each hollow lived more like a ditch.
I've been seduced and I've been stung;
I've been the woman who has hung
up on herself, maliciously.
These are the words to which I've clung:
no woman gets through life for free.

Cleaned up the scattered shards I've flung,
picked up my bags, my dark debris.
What have I learned, when all is slung?
No woman gets through life for free.

About the Author

Allison Joseph is the author of five full-length collections of poetry, *What Keeps Us Here* (Ampersand, 1992), *Soul Train* (Carnegie Mellon, 1997), *In Every Seam* (University of Pittsburgh Press, 1997), *Imitation of Life* (Carnegie Mellon, 2003) and *Worldly Pleasures* (Word Press, 2004). Her poems are often attuned to the experiences of women and minorities. *What Keeps Us Here* was the winner of Ampersand Press' 1992 Women Poets Series Competition. It also received the John C. Zacharis First Book Award from *Ploughshares* and Emerson College in Boston. In addition, she was awarded Illinois Arts Council Fellowships in Poetry in 1996 and 2007 and a Literary Award from the Illinois Arts Council in 1997. Her poems have appeared in *Ploughshares, Callaloo, Parnassus, The Southern Review,* and *The Kenyon Review.* Other honors include the 2001 Nonfiction Award from the Peralta Press literary journal, the Illinois winner in the Rock River Times Poetry Contest VI, and awards from the poetry societies of New Hampshire and Pennsylvania. Allison holds degrees from Kenyon College and Indiana University. Currently she is an Associate Professor at Southern Illinois University, Carbondale, where she serves as editor for *Crab Orchard Review* and director of the Young Writers Workshop, a summer conference for high school-aged writers.

Other Recent Titles from Mayapple Press:

Josie Kearns, *The Theory of Everything*, 2008
        Paper, 86 pp, $14.95 plus s&h
        ISBN 978-0932412-744
Eleanor Lerman, *The Blonde on the Train*, 2008
        Paper, 164 pp, $16.95 plus s&h
        ISBN 978-0932412-737
Sophia Rivkin, *The Valise*, 2008
        Paper, 38 pp, $12.95 plus s&h
        ISBN 978-0932412-720
Alice George, *This Must Be the Place*, 2008
        Paper, 48 pp, $12.95 plus s&h
        ISBN 978-0932412-713
Angela Williams, *Live from the Tiki Lounge*, 2008
        Paper, 48 pp, $12.95 plus s&h
        ISBN 978-0932412-706
Claire Keyes, *The Question of Rapture*, 2008
        Paper, 72 pp, $14.95 plus s&h
        ISBN 978-0932412-690
Judith Kerman and Amee Schmidt, eds., *Greenhouse: The First 5 Years
of the Rustbelt Roethke Writers' Workshop*, 2008
        Paper, 78 pp, $14.95 plus s&h
        ISBN 978-0932412-683
Cati Porter, *Seven Floors Up*, 2008
        Paper, 66 pp, $14.95 plus s&h
        ISBN 978-0932412-676
Rabbi Manes Kogan, *Fables from the Jewish Tradition*, 2008
        Paper, 104 pp, $19.95 plus s&h
        ISBN 978-0932412-669
Joy Gaines-Friedler, *Like Vapor*, 2008
        Paper, 64 pp, $14.95 plus s&h
        ISBN 978-0932412-652
Jane Piirto, *Saunas*, 2008
        Paper, 100 pp, $15.95 plus s&h
        ISBN 978-0932412-645
Joel Thomas Katz, *Away*, 2008
        Paper, 42 pp, $12.95 plus s&h
        ISBN 978-0932412-638

For a complete catalog of Mayapple Press publications, please visit our website at *www.mayapplepress.com.* Books can be ordered direct from our website with secure on-line payment using PayPal, or by mail (check or money order). Or order through your local bookseller.